FOOD FORMULAS

FOR

HUNGRY NEANDERTHALS

Also by Vera Dragilyova

LUCID DREAMS

INTUITIVE MEDICINE

UNIVERSAL LANGUAGE BASE

THE BEST OF ALL WORLDS

FOOD FORMULAS

FOR

HUNGRY NEANDERTHALS

Ancient Recipes From Around the World

Vera Dragilyova

Verarta Books

CONTENTS

Introduction   1

A Thought for food   3
Quick and easy to prepare   7
Maximum nutritional value   8
Purity and freshness   8
Gustatory pleasure   10
Open air   11

Ingredients   13

Food Formulas   49
Whole dishes   54
Paste dishes   55
Spread dishes   57
Folded dishes   58
Encased dishes   59
Rolled dishes   59
Sandwich   61
Toppings   63
Drink mixes   64
Soup   66
Salad   73
Curry   78
Stir fry   79

INTRODUCTION

What to eat? A question as old as humanity itself. It is a decision we make on the daily basis, and one that determines how long we live and how happy we are all along. The value of food in our lives is influenced by the aesthetic experience and nutrition the food provides, determining both our longevity and lifelong joy.

However, this is not a cook book. It is rather an attempt at breaking down the DNA code of dishes, outlining their basic parts that have been preserved through the millennia of human migration, all around the planet. The book does not talk about every single food ingredient available to Homo Sapiens, nor does it cover every cooking method and recipe that ever existed in the history of the world. Instead, it takes a structural approach at examining at the world's cuisine.

I

It appears that food practices migrated across the planet along the human routes that have long been erased from the earth's memory. Central Asian plov became tajin in North Africa, and paella in Spain. This is not about looking for the proof, but only about noticing structural patterns in human dishes, and digging through to the roots of cooking buried deep in history—probably, from the time we lived alongside Neanderthals.

A THOUGHT FOR FOOD

You are what you eat. You eat what you cook. You cook what you choose to buy at the market. So, essentially, you buy yourself at the market. Just a thought... Yesterday I ate such a tasty piece of meat, it was the best chocolate I ever had!

On a serious note, I don't eat food per pound, I measure food in units of pleasure. And a pleasure in eating is multi-faceted, appealing to all of the five human senses. The presentation of food, its colors and apparent texture—all either invites or deters one from desiring it. After all, consuming food is a sexual act, in that it is intrusive, intimate, and mutual, sustaining our life and providing us with continuous rebirth, on the cellular level. Smell is an ancient and powerful indicator that controls food appeal: one can smell a good bakery from miles away, and instantly melt into a comfort zone.

3

Our eyes were very good at telling us what was good for us, until modern technology learned how to dupe them, making dishes look good, but taste like nothing, and have little to no nutritional value.

When we chew our food, we do not only feel its taste and texture, but we also hear it, as the sound travels through our flesh and bones, into our eardrums, just as the outside world is entering our body through what we eat, and thereby becomes us.

The aesthetic experience of food consumption will differ from person to person, just like each cook creates something different, even when the recipe is exactly the same. Altitude, temperature, humidity, cookware—all drastically influence one's cooking, and so does one's emotional state. Some people have a green thumb, and some have a "cooking thumb": whatever they touch comes out tasty.

Eating is living, and cooking is really about creating life. It is like constantly producing

4

offspring, except you eat it yourself: a phantasmagoric circle of life that is beautiful and empowering. Seeing it that way heightens one's awareness of the present, past, and future, and provides an intense meaning in life.

What is the secret? Wishing well and giving yourself to the process is the answer. Watch your food develop and feel its properties and proportions with your hands and eyes, instead of blindly following a recipe. Just like always relying on GPS will not let you learn the route and will actually get you lost if technology fails, so always following a recipe, without feeling out the whole process, will not make you into a good cook. Just like driving on your own will get you lost and found, the route never forgotten, so your cooking flops will make your cooking a personal and unique experience, making both preparation and consumption much more meaningful and enjoyable.

The goal is not to make a perfect dish, but a dish that is perfectly yours, one that you love—so that others will fall in love with it, too. Just like in the movie "Like Water for Chocolate",—meaning boiling hot—Tita cooks her tears into the food, making the guests cry when the eat it, so can you cook all the love and care into your dishes, coming from your heart, through your hands, and directly into the people who eat your food. Cooking for yourself and others is like playing God: it is designing human being from the inside, in the most tacit, yet, the most powerful of ways.

Besides the emotional component of cooking well, there are several principles by which I guide my cooking practice. They all appeal to how early humans must have lived, cooked and eaten, at least, according to the archeological findings. I find their ways both aesthetically pleasing and good for health.

Quick and easy to prepare.

My first principle is: throw it all together and watch it cook itself! Minimal food handling yields results that are both aesthetically pleasing and good for health. It is true that many vegetables increase their nutritional value with heat exposure, but generally, overcooking kills nutrients. Over-handled food is food that required too much contact with hands, too many steps in preparation that takes too long, so that the resulting dish stops resembling its original ingredients. When I eat something, I want immediately to taste where the ingredients came from and what they are. In overhanded food, freshness and nutrients have been lost in the process. The shorter and less intrusive the cooking process—the better. Asian cuisine, generally, follows this principle. Traditional Asian food is quick to prepare, and virtually everyone always knows what they are eating—because the form of the original ingredients is well preserved and not over-handled.

Quick and easy becomes urgently important, when one is leading a modern lifestyle: it may make a difference between cooking or not cooking at all, and having to eat out, relegating the creation of your body through food into a stranger's hands.

Maximum nutritional value.

When shopping, I refer to my list of ingredients—foods that I want to eat for the vitamins they contain. I don't venture outside this list, which ensures that I eat healthy. My focus has always been on proteins and vegetables, fruit, berries, and unprocessed ingredients readily found in nature. This is what our ancestors did for millennia.

Purity and freshness.

Nutritional value of ingredients can be undone, if they contain toxins, or if they are not fresh. Toxins poison our bodies. Before the chemical industry took agriculture under its wing, organic and non-GMO food used to be the norm, and now we are forced to seek them out, as if they are something special: only because the new normal is toxic.

Cooking with utensils that leak toxins into the food is just as bad. Using glass, ceramic and wooden utensils, and avoiding all types of plastics helps maintain purity. Using traditional methods of cooking, such as heating in the oven or boiling, and avoiding using a microwave, also helps preserve the original nutrition value of the ingredients.

Old and stale food is overgrown with noxious bacteria, and food like that should not be consumed, since it is literally poisonous. In more traditional cultures, leftovers are not a common practice, even when refrigeration is available.

Fruit and vegetables that are picked locally and in season are the best to consume, especially when the time between their harvesting and consumption is kept to a minimum. This is how our ancestors lived: picking fruit and berries and eating them right then and there, and cooking their hunting trophies as soon as they arrived back home.

Gustatory pleasure.

On the basis of all the most nutritive, pure, and fresh ingredients, I create dishes that provide maximum pleasure when consumed. That way, I combine nutrition with a pleasant experience: but nutrition must come first. Pleasure in food is essential: that is how our body knows that it is good for it, and it is the easiest way to experience daily joy—if everything else fails. Plus, tasty food makes people chew slower, which leads to better digestion, and better health.

Open air.

Eating outside, on the fresh air, with bare feet, and eating with one's hands, without using metal utensils, is the most pleasurable and healthy way to eat. Using wooden chopsticks is ok, but metal silverware? Not really. Especially knives and forks: those have sharp edges and create an atmosphere of aggression and danger.

INGREDIENTS

There are three main determinants of taste in food: water, salt, and the nutrients drawn by the plants from the soil, and animals from the food they eat. That is, provided, that the ingredients are fresh or properly aged.

Water pH factor determines much of its taste, but there is also texture, which is created by the mineral content, and how big the mineral particles are. "Softer" water will have fewer or finer minerals. Some water tastes fresh and almost sweet, and feels decisively good for health. My favorite water is sourced in Fiji: it is just fresh and soft enough to make it taste like liquid air.

Salt should be considered a spice, because it has such a complex taste capacity. It is not a spice, because it is a mineral, and does not come from a plant. Sea salt, to my taste, has the most complex flavor, because of the trace minerals contained in it, besides pure sodium chloride. The taste of salt determines the overall taste of a dish. Some sweet dishes, such as good old cookies, also contain salt, which determines their taste complexity and the aesthetic gustatory experience.

Food that is stale or full of chemicals usually acquires a sour taste, or metallic aftertaste, when it involves rancid oil,—or even bitterness. Fresh, organic food tastes somewhat sweet compared to that, and can have subtle notes of grasses and flowers in fruit and vegetables.

The following is a shortlist of foods that I use in cooking, in order to get the fullest range of nutrition. When in doubt at a grocery store, I just refer to this list, instead of being swayed by ads and thoughtful product placement.

A great indicator of good quality in fruit and vegetables is their strong pleasant aroma. An absence of aroma signifies either their not being ripe, or their having been grown on depleted soil, and a consequent lack of nutrients that should otherwise be there. Proteins, on the other hand, should have minimum aroma, look taut and feel somewhat springy to touch. If there is a slimy residue on them—they are too old and should not be consumed.

Oils

Olive oil—vitamins E, A, K, potassium, magnesium, calcium, and iron. I use virgin, unrefined, cold-pressed oil only, and the most flavorful varieties are found in Portugal. Greek varieties come second, and Italian varieties take the third place. Unrefined olive oil is not meant to be heated, because it can become toxic with relatively little heating. It is best to use it in salads, on hummus, and in any cold dish.

Grapeseed oil—vitamin E and antioxidants. This is the best oil for cooking rice. Without it, my rice comes out too dry, and each grain comes out rickety, but with it—each grain will have smooth edges and will have a springy quality to it. Smothering chicken, fish and meats with grapeseed oil before cooking will usually preserve the natural juices and prevent the protein from drying out and shriveling.

Coconut oil, unrefined and refined—vitamin E and long-chain fatty acids. Good for frying and in hot dishes, since it solidifies at room temperature, becoming unpleasant for consumption in that form. The refined oil has no coconut aroma, while unrefined—does. Coconut aroma, in my opinion, goes better with anything that is non-savory.

Palm oil, red and unrefined—very high on vitamin E. Used for frying or in protein and vegetable dishes, to add color. The oil has a slightly bitter taste, especially when heated. Frying eggs with red palm oil is great fun.

Sesame oil, unrefined and toasted—copper, zinc, iron, calcium and magnesium. It is very flavorful, and I prefer it in a salad dressing and stir fries. It endows proteins with a deep aroma note, when they are cooked in heat.

Peanut oil, unrefined and toasted—vitamin E and phytosterols, good for the heart. It has a pleasant nutty flavor, and I use it in salads and stir fries, as well as with baking or frying proteins.

Proteins

Duck—vitamin B12. Duck is a body heating meat, and it is one of the best foods to eat, when one has a cold or a flu, or just during cold weather. I love to pair duck with something sweet like apples, pears, or prunes, and bake it all together. Cinnamon spice goes well with duck. Best with fat present.

Beef—iron, zinc, selenium, thiamine, riboflavin, niacin, vitamin B6 and B12, vitamin D, phosphorus, pantothenate, magnesium and potassium. Beef seems to help with confidence and drive,—but that is off the record. Best with fat present. One of my favorite beef dishes is cow tail stew, with onions and carrots. It a very gelatinous dish, which is very good for the nails, skin and hair.

Beef liver—vitamin A, B12, riboflavin, folate, iron, copper, choline. Eating liver is actually good for one's liver. Beef liver is widely eaten in the Middle

East, North Africa and also Asia, but less in the West.

Pork—vitamin B6, thiamin, phosphorus, niacin, selenium, zinc, riboflavin and potassium. Pork seems to stabilize emotions and wards off neurotic thoughts—again, off the record.

Turkey—niacin, vitamin B6 and B12, tryptophan, zinc. Because of tryptophan, turkey meat helps to improve one's mood and sleep, by affecting serotonin levels.

Chicken, thigh meat—vitamin B complex, magnesium, potassium, phosphorus, and zinc. Chicken meat heats up the body, similar to the duck, but has a slightly softer effect. No wonder, it is chicken soup that everyone recommends for getting rid of a cold. I like baked chicken with mushrooms, prunes and onions, chicken schnitzel, or chicken rolls with greens, cheese, and nuts on the inside. Cinnamon is an excellent spice for chicken, as long as it is not overbearing: the most subtle the better. In fact, in Morocco, there is chicken dish called bstilla, that uses nuts and cinnamon with pulled chicken in flaky dough, and with powdered sugar on top.

Chicken liver—very high vitamin A, vitamin B complex, especially B-12, folate. In the post-Soviet region, chicken liver is made into a paste, with an addition of fried onions and garlic, and served on bread, or mixed with egg yokes and stuffed into boiled egg whites.

Salmon—Omega 3. Salmon, just like any fish and most seafood has a cooling effect on the body, and is not recommended during colds. At least, that is what they say in Egypt—and it has worked for me. Since salmon contains a lot of natural oils, I don't add any at all in cooking, except maybe a few drops of a flavorful olive oil from Portugal. The spice thyme goes well with cooked salmon, and dried dill is good for smoked salmon. I use hot-smoked salmon mixed with cream cheese, to make a spread. Tartar sauce and avocado go well with salmon, too.

Shrimp—vitamin B-12, phosphorus, choline, copper, iodine. I like paprika or fresh chopped basil with shrimp, or simply thyme and black pepper. Tartar sauce and avocado go well with shrimp.

Clams—high on iron, but also selenium, zinc, magnesium and B complex. I prefer smoked baby clams for their intense taste and non-chewy texture.

Oysters— high in zinc, but also iron, selenium, and **vitamins** B12 and D. Like with clams, I prefer cooked smoked oysters, and never eat them raw, to avoid food poisoning.

Eggs, especially yoke—choline, vitamins A, D, E and K, Omega-3.

Spices

Spices have a strong association with ancient cooking. Real spices, and not artificial flavors of the modern age. I noticed that, within my favorite traditional spices, there are groups, based on color: red, green, brown, yellow and white:

Red: paprika and cayenne pepper.
Green: thyme, oregano, cardamon, tarragon, cloves, mint.
Brown: cumin, coriander, cinnamon, nutmeg, allspice.
Yellow: turmeric.

The colors somehow correlate with the aroma—just like perfumes. Brown spices have the deepest notes, then yellow, then red, and only then —the green that feel the highest. Spices with brown notes usually linger longer in a dish and are not easily distorted with heat. Spices with green notes feel higher on the aroma spectrum, do not linger as long with a dish, and are easier to destroy with heat.

Cumin, whole seeds—vitamins A, E, C, K, B6, magnesium, iron, calcium and phosphorous. Great in quinoa, but also vegetables and ground proteins.

Caraway, whole seeds—an anti-bacterial. Great for rice and quinoa, vegetable stir fries, breads, ground proteins.

Fennel, whole—vitamin C, calcium, magnesium, potassium, and manganese. They are great on eggplant.

Garlic, granulated—a superfood, fantastic for the immune function. Garlic is a universal spice, good on anything savory.

Onion, granulated—great for the immune function, and is a universal spice like granulated garlic. To me, it adds an umami taste the for dishes.

Chives, fresh and dried—potassium, iron and calcium, vitamins A and C, folate, niacin, riboflavin and thiamin. Just like granulated garlic and onion, chives can add a certain depth to the aroma and taste of a dish, but it is greener and does not withstand heat very well. Chive can be decorative on soups, salads, meats, and just about anything savory.

Powdered spices

Cumin—vitamins A, E, C, K, B6, magnesium, iron, calcium and phosphorous. I love it on hummus and on fried eggs.

Coriander—vitamin C and K. A universal spice for savory dishes.

Turmeric—a superfood, antibacterial and antiviral, can be used on fried eggs and in coconut curries. Adds a strong yellow coloration to the dish.

Cayenne pepper—great for digestion, adds a subtle spice if used sparingly. A universal spicer for anything sweet or savory!

Black pepper—anti-inflammatory, good for the heart, blood sugar, and cholesterol. This is another universal spicer.

Oregano—anti-bacterial, antiviral, great for the immune function. A green and decorative spice, especially good on eggs, chicken, shrimp, and just about anything, really. Widely used in Italian cuisine.

Thyme—vitamin A, C, copper, fiber, iron, and manganese. Thyme is great with all seafood, but also works with meat and chicken.

25

Cinnamon—anti-inflammatory, good for blood sugar, full of antioxidants. In tiny amounts, it makes chicken and duck irresistible! A little secret ingredient that is not detected, but adds a deep note that mades a dish sound a symphony inside your brain.

Cardamon—immune function, antibacterial, good for digestion. Just like cloves, it has a strong green flavor, and is an exception to the green family of spices, in that it has deep green notes that overpower almost any other spice. Great in coconut curries.

Paprika—vitamin A, E, B6. I love it on shrimp and in cooked bell pepper salad.

Nutmeg—vitamin B complex, good for digestion, brain, and the sleep. It adds very deep stone notes to a dish, and is good for stews with beef, especially cow tail stew.

Allspice—vitamin C, iron, magnesium, potassium and copper. It is a magic ingredient that transforms a meat dish into something out of this world—only if used in small amounts, because it can easily become overpowering. Widely used in Jamaican cuisine.

Tarragon—good for the heart and blood sugar, helps better sleep, anti-inflammatory. Great on shrimp, beef, chicken. In the country of Georgia, a sweet drink is made with fresh tarragon leaves.

Lavender—reduces stress and helps sleep. It is great in chicken dishes, in small quantities, so as not to overpower the overall flavor. It can also be used as a tea, especially before sleep.

Cloves—liver health, blood sugar, digestion, antibacterial. It is great in coconut curries, and has to be used carefully, so as not to overpower the overall flavor of a dish.

Mesquite powder—E, D, C, Niacin, B6, and folic acid. It is essentially carob, but grown in Peru, less sweet than carob, and adds smokey sweetness. Great in chicken and meat dishes. Also can be used in sweet dishes.

Spice-like ingredients

Nutritional yeast—very high vitamin B complex, for salads and salad dressing. Has a calming effect on the mind.

Dry mushroom powders: porcini, matsutake, truffles—immune system, for any savory dish.

Kelp, dry flakes—iodine, for Asian dishes, rice and eggs.

Fresh garlic paste—immune system, for all dishes, except drinks.

Fresh ginger paste—immune system, digestion, for all dishes and drinks.

Grains

Rice—protein, basmati and jasmine, white. Brown rice has too much arsenic and takes longer too cook.

Quinoa—essential amino acids, fiber, magnesium, B vitamins, iron, potassium, calcium, phosphorus, vitamin E.

Buckwheat—vitamins B2 and B3, phosphorus, zinc, iron, calcium, potassium, selenium, magnesium, manganese.

Lentils

Yellow and black—vitamin B complex, iron, magnesium, potassium and zinc.

Yellow—for soups, black—for soups and to be mixed with rice.

Seeds

Sesame seeds, unbleached—zinc, selenium, copper, iron, vitamin B6 and E. Sesame seeds are great for decorating of all kinds: it could be mixed into a paste or liquid where it is visible, or sprinkled on top of salads, hummus, meats, eggs, and more. They add a subtle pleasant taste to both savory and sweet dishes.

Black cumin seeds—iron, copper, zinc, phosphorus, calcium, thiamin, niacin, pyridoxine, and folic acid. They are more intense than sesame seeds, but look almost identical.

Pumpkin seeds—iron, calcium, B2, folate and beta-carotene, which is a precursor to vitamin A. I like them with salads, stir fries, and all kinds of proteins, except shellfish and liver. They have a very subtle taste, but their texture is pleasant, especially when they are already roasted or have been cooked for a while. Could be used both in sweet and savory dishes.

Sunflower seeds—vitamin B complex, phosphorus, magnesium, iron, calcium, potassium, protein, and vitamin E. I use them in the same way as pumpkin seeds—in everything. Could be used both in sweet and savory dishes.

Watermelon seeds, fresh and dried—vitamin B complex, proteins, folate, iron, zinc, copper, magnesium, potassium. These seeds are hard to find in dried form, but they are easily found in their fresh form inside a seeded watermelon. They are great to eat fresh! Watermelon seeds are used in cuisine all over Western Africa.

Berries

Raspberries—vitamin C and good for women's health. Tea with raspberry jam is used in Eastern Europe to lower a fever.

Strawberries—vitamin C, folate, manganese, potassium. There is no better berry in the world that mixes better into sweet recipes, especially those involving milk products. Strawberries should have no white streaks on the inside, if they are organic.

Blueberries—vitamin K1, vitamin C, manganese, and bioflavonoids.

Maqui, dried powder—a superfruit, vitamins A and C, calcium, iron, potassium, and very high in bioflavonoids. I use this powder in yogurt, but it can be used in any sweet recipe, adding a strong dark purple tint to the food.

Goji berries, dried powder—vitamin A, C, iron, copper, selenium, and very high in antioxidants. Dried goji berries are very tough to eat, so a good solution is to consume them in a powder form. They naturally have a sweetness to them, and an orange color that they add to the food. Just like maqui berries, I use them in yogurts, but they can be used in any sweet dishes.

Mulberries, fresh and dried—vitamin C, E, K1, iron, and potassium. Mulberries are rarely sold in their fresh form, simply because they are very fragile and spoil very quickly. To eat them fresh, one should pick them off a tree. Some farmer's markets sell them, because they are able to get them to the public, quickly after they are picked. Usually, it is the dry variety that is available at a store, and they are rather tough. In their dry form, they can be used in sweet recipes, especially liquid ones, where mulberries will soak and soften.

Cherries—potassium, calcium, vitamin A and folic acid. Tart cherries are tart, but the blander varieties are easily eaten fresh. Dried cherries are not too sweet, not too sour, and are easy to use in any savory or sweet recipe: salads, meat, chicken, duck.

Fresh herbs

Cilantro—is the green leaf of coriander, the spice powder that is made of dried coriander seeds. It has potassium, manganese, choline, beta-carotene (precursor to vitamin A), folate, and more.

Rosemary—vitamin A, B6, C, folate. I love fresh rosemary on young potatoes. It is a strong herb and should be used carefully.

Basil—vitamin A, C, K, manganese, iron, calcium, magnesium, Omega-3. It pairs well with tomatoes, but also with any chicken and meat dishes. Widely used in both Thai and Italian cuisine.

Mint—a super herb, great for digestion. Can be used universally, in all dishes.

Ginger—immune system, digestion, a superfood. Can be used universally, in all dishes, but can be overpowering.

Nuts

Pistachios—vitamin B6, phosphorus, copper, manganese. Best for sweet dishes.

Peanuts—protein, fiber, potassium, phosphorous, magnesium, and B vitamins. Great in peanut butter. In the West—used mostly in sweet dishes, and in Asia—in savory dishes, especially in Thailand.

Walnuts—vitamin B6, magnesium, Omega 3. Dry walnuts are good in meats and chicken dishes, and in all sweet dishes. Green walnuts are widely eaten in the region between Turkey and Eastern Europe.

They are crunchy and have a very different taste from the dry ones: it is hauntingly umami-like!

Pecans—antioxidants, manganese, potassium, calcium, iron, magnesium, zinc, and selenium. They are best for sweet dishes, and have a maple-like taste that adds richness to any sweet dish.

Macadamia—vitamin A, iron, protein, thiamine, riboflavin and niacin. They are best eaten alone or in sweet dishes. Both Hawaii and Australia are famous for their macadamias, but originate in Australia.

Pine nuts—vitamin B complex, vitamin K, phosphorus, magnesium, zinc and manganese. They are best in cold dishes, such as hummus and salads. Some of the most flavorful pine nuts are found in Russia.

Sweeteners

Xylitol granules—kills bad bacteria in the body. Originally derived from birch tree juice. Has very low glycemic index, which is good for regulating blood sugar, and has a mild taste, not irritating like that of sugar from the sugarcane. Can be used instead of sugar.

Carob syrup—digestion, vitamins E, D, C, Niacin, B6, and folic acid. A dark and deep sweetener, with slight bitter and sour notes. Avoid using in drinks, but great everywhere else.

Yacon syrup—a prebiotic, good for the good bacteria in the gut. Has a mild, fruity taste, and can be used everywhere except drinks, where it acquires a certain unpleasant acidity.

Molasses—iron, calcium, magnesium, vitamin B-6, selenium. This is essentially a concentrate of all the nutrients that are stripped off of sugar, as it is derived from sugar can and turned into white powder.

Honey—supports immune function, antibacterial, antiviral, and much more. This is a universal sweetener, and can be used in all dishes, from sweet to savory, from dry to liquid, from cold to hot. There are many varieties of honey, and each one has its own best uses.

Herbal tea

Chamomile—good for relaxation, sleep, and digestion.

Green tea—great for energy and weight loss, antioxidants, and a very small amount of caffeine. Japanese varieties of green tea are my favorite. They are the lightest and greenest, matcha being the greenest of them all.

Lavender—relaxation and sleep, antibacterial. Lavender can be overpowering, so it is best when either used in small quantities, or as addition to another herbal tea. One only has to visit the lavender fields in the south of France to appreciate this amazing herb.

Mint—digestion, antibacterial, immune function. Mint adds a tiny bit of spice into a drink, and tends to turn dark brown in hot liquid—in both dry or fresh forms, so it can stain teeth. Adding lemon to the drink will bleach it instantly.

Hibiscus—to lower pressure, sour and needs a sweetener. A deep bluish red in color, this is a traditional drink of Egypt, from the times of the Pharaohs.

Rooibos—antioxidants, good for the heart. Grown in South Africa, and is orange-brown in color.

Rose hips—high in vitamin C. It can taste bitter and sour, and has to be sweetened.

Calendula—antibacterial, anti-fungal, anti-inflammatory. It is made of marigold flowers, and has a pleasantly bitter-fruity and subtle taste.

Soursop—a great anti-cancer preventative remedy. It has a very mild taste, and is best paired with a stronger-flavored herb.

Chrysanthemum—for blood pressure, diabetes, and immune system health. The tea consists of beautiful light yellow flowers that open up in hot water, so serving the tea in clear glass containers is a spectacular must.

Fruit

Watermelon—vitamin A, B6, C, antioxidants.

Cantaloupe—high in vitamin A and C.

Apples—an apple a day keeps the doctor away. Vitamin A and C, vitamin B complex, folate.

Pears—vitamin A and C, vitamin B complex, folate.

Apricots—vitamin A and C, vitamin B complex, folate.

Prickly pears—vitamin A and C, vitamin B complex, magnesium, potassium, calcium, copper, fiber.

Asian pears—vitamin C and K, potassium, copper.

Pomegranates—vitamin B, C, and K, potassium, folate. Great when eaten with seeds, which cleanse the gut.

Peaches, especially flat Asian variety—vitamin A, vitamin B complex, vitamin C, K, and potassium.

Oranges—vitamin A and C, vitamin B complex, folate.

Pineapple—vitamin C, bromelain for digestion.

Lemons—vitamin C, weight loss, bromeliad for digestion.

Lime—goes well on papaya, vitamin C, weight loss, digestion.

Papaya—goes well with lime juice, vitamin A, digestion and weight loss.

Prunes—potassium, iron, slightly laxative.

Vegetables

Onion—vitamin B6 and C, potassium, folate, great for immune system.

Garlic—vitamin B6 and C, potassium, phosphorous, copper, manganese, great for immune system.

Brussel sprouts—vitamin B6, C, K, potassium, fiber, thiamine, magnesium, phosphorus.

Asparagus—vitamins A, C, K, chromium, fiber, folate, good for blood sugar.

Artichokes—vitamins C, K, folate, fiber, potassium, magnesium, phosphorous. Good for kidneys.

Okra—vitamins A, B6, C, thiamin, folate, calcium, magnesium, manganese, phosphorous, potassium, zinc, copper.

Carrots—high in vitamin A, B6, and K1. Good for the eyes.

Potatoes—high in vitamin C, B6, potassium, magnesium, fiber, antioxidants.

Tomatoes—vitamins A, K, vitamin B complex, and vitamin C.

Cucumbers—vitamins A, C, K, magnesium, potassium, manganese.

Eggplant—vitamin C, vitamin K, vitamin B6, thiamine, niacin, magnesium, manganese, phosphorus, copper, fiber, folic acid, potassium.

Bell peppers—vitamins A, C, potassium.

Radish—vitamin B6, K, calcium, folate, potassium.

Beets—vitamin C, folate, manganese, potassium, iron. Great for detoxification, acne, and weight loss.

Avocado—vitamin B complex, high in potassium, magnesium.

Cabbage—high in vitamins C and K, fiber. Great for kidneys.

Vinegar

Rice vinegar—antioxidants.

Apple cider vinegar—vitamin B complex, vitamin C, antibacterial, anti-inflammatory, weight loss, hearth health and cholesterol.

Salad greens

Arugula—vitamin A, C, K, folate, magnesium, calcium.

Watercress—vitamin A, C, E, K, B6, folate, iron and iodine.

Juices

Birch tree juice—contains xylitol, great antibacterial, works on cellulite.

Coconut water—electrolytes, immune system, a superfood.

Tart cherry—urinary tract, antibacterial, weight loss. Best mixed with bubbly water, to soften the tartness.

Fresh mushrooms

Maitake—immune function, longevity.

Shiitake—immune function, heart.

Lion's Maine—vitamin B complex, brain, mood improvement, digestion, heart, diabetes.

Oyster mushrooms—vitamin B complex, vitamin C, D, folic acid, calcium, iron, zinc, potassium, phosphorus, selenium, fiber, protein.

Crimini—vitamin B complex, phosphorous, potassium, zinc, copper, manganese, selenium.

All of these ingredients are of natural origins, and the closest to the earth, with no processing, except maybe nutritional yeast and granulated garlic and onion.

FOOD FORMULAS

Although the number of dishes that exists in the world seems to be limitless, there are only so many structural ways that food is cooked by humans. For example, we don't vaporize food and then inhale it, we don't spread it so thin that it becomes invisible, and we don't make it into jewelry to be eaten. On another thought,—edible jewelry! Hm, that's an idea! I wouldn't mind having a collier made of bright cherries. Hungry? Food is conveniently nearby. How about a belt made of sausage? How about earrings in the shape of tiny plastic bags, filled with orange juice? Thirsty? I've got it all right here.

So, where does real cooking begin? Is it with cutting an ingredient, or only when something is heated that it qualifies to be a dish? Is a piece of meat, grilled over fire, a dish? Is a chopped bell pepper a dish? If a fruit is picked off a tree, has it become a dish now? It seems that there is a continuum, from minimal to intricate human work involved in cooking. On one end of the spectrum, we have a fruit that we eat whole, just picked off a tree—an apple, say. We had to pull it off the branch —so, maybe, that is somehow cooking? Well, some will say that raw vs. cooked is a good heuristic to tell the difference, but a raw salad seems to be a cooked dish, somehow, just because there is cutting and mixing involved. On the other end of the spectrum, we have a soup—the most cooked dish possible, because it usually involved chopping, mixing, boiling, and prolonged heat. Even slow barbecue over fire seems somehow less cooked than a soup. Food, perhaps, is the most varied activity of all the activities that humankind has engaged in, during its entire history.

In order to start experimenting with creating one's own food, one needs no formulas, really. However, having some reference is a good start for those who care to stay somewhat close to the traditions. Formulas are also a reference for seeing a big picture, illustrating the totality of human cuisine: what is still not there, and what still could be! Maybe someone can design a fundamentally different dish that has never been cooked before. In order to break the rules, one must know what they are.

There are flowers and there are leaves in every dish. Flowers is sine qua non of a dish, the center of attention and excitement, without which the meal could not exist. Leaves are secondary and non-essential, without which the meal could still "go on", like a show. For some people the flower is meat, and vegetables are leaves. For some people, dessert is the flower, and everything else is leaves. A food formula lists the flowers first, and leaves come next.

All dishes we know appear to follow certain patterns and canons of food-making. It looks like each dish can be classified according to three parameters: dry/liquid, hot/cold, and structure:

toppings, whole, mixed, stuffed, paste, rolled, spread, sandwich, fold, encased, where the last five are really variations of the same basic structure of pizza,—with a cover and a filling. A cover is usually tougher and more protective, while the filling is usually softer, and protected by the cover. I cannot think of any dish that has a structure of a peach, which is the opposite—with a soft cover and a hard core.

An example of a dry dish is shish kebab—pieces of meat cooked over fire or grilled, with no sauce added. Classical fried rice is probably a dry dish, too. Wet foods are soups, stews, and drinks, of course. A mixture of dry and wet is something like a salad with a dressing. The hotter and the wetter the dish, the more of a dish it is, it seems. For example, cold slices of salami and cheese—is that a dish? Yes, only somewhat. It is cold and dry.

A stew or a soup is definitely a dish, however. Salads are mixed dishes, so is fried rice, stir fries, curries, and soups. Majority of dishes are mixed, it seems. Even those that contain only one main ingredient, usually come in a paste, like Middle-Eastern hummus (made of primarily chickpeas), or baba ganuj (made of eggplant). And even in those dishes—no one in reality uses one single ingredient, and oil, lemon juice, sesame paste and spices are virtually always added to them. How about sesame paste, tahini? Is that a dish? It is rather an ingredient, and not a dish. How do we know what is an ingredient and what is a dish? An ingredient would not be normally eaten on its own, but a dish usually is.

Of course, some people even eat raw potatoes, and ingredients, whether raw or cooked, can be consumed on their own, but it is human traditions that determine what is a dish and what is not. For example, in cultures close to the North Pole, people consume raw meat, completely on its own, and for them—it is a dish. It is not even cooked, barely cut, but in their culture—it is a dish. Some cultures consider a meal incomplete without a

53

hot soup—Russian and Chinese traditional culture are examples.

Whole dishes

Whole dishes are solid, dry, with one main ingredient, and not in a form paste. An example of whole structure dish is pieces of meat cooked over fire, or a Spanish dried and aged pork leg that is sliced. Those are on the borderline with being ingredients, if people use them in sandwiches or necessarily eat them with foods. Whole dishes are more common in the north of Russia and Asia, among Native Indians, in Polynesia, Australia, and among the original inhabitants of the Americas. You can still see remnant of that form in German and Poland, and in Scandinavia, as well as Greenland, with their rotten fish. Original hunter populations seem to specialize in that kind of dishes.

Paste dishes

With the exception of mashed potatoes and blended soups, dishes in the form of a paste are relatively rare in Europe, Asia, and the Americas, but are more common in Africa and India, and the Middle East, some spreading into Northern Africa. Africa is a center for all kinds of paste, as well as mixed foods. Ugali, a famous maize flower porridge eaten in Kenya, is a perfect example. All kinds of porridge are available all throughout Africa, and it seems that foods in the form of paste are typical of settled populations that have been able to cultivate a crop. India is very similar to Africa in its predominant food structures—it is all about paste and stew in Southern India, Sri Lanka, and Maldives. Only in the Northern India, we get whole structure with grilled meat.

Paste dishes are often made of beans or eggplant, and they are usually eaten with other vegetables or with bread, or meat. Another type of paste dishes are dips and sauces, but those are even more dependent on other dishes for their existence. Generally, a sauce is an auxiliary to a dry dish, usually in chunks or pieces of grilled, or deep-fried meat or vegetables, or bread, or chips. A dip is the same as a sauce, but it is not poured over another dish, but sits still, while another food is dipped into it. Because of that, dips can be much thicker than sauces. A salad dressing is basically a thinner sauce, thin enough so that it can easily spread over the salad ingredients.

A typical sauce, dip, or a bean/eggplant dish is made of oil or water, a base, which can consist of ground nuts or seeds, spices, sweeteners, beans, and almost any food ingredient, really. What defines a paste dish is its texture and consistency. Thicker paste dishes are usually dips, humus, and eggplant-based baba ganuj. All of them can be served with an indentation in the middle, where one can put some nuts, ground meat, or finely sliced vegetables, in order to make it more interesting.

My favorite dish from this group is hummus with ground lamb and pine nuts, with some sprinkled cumin spice on top. It is a dish from Yemen.

Spread dishes

The most obvious representative of this group is Italian pizza. It has relatives around the world. Native American Indian pizza is probably older, just like structurally identical dishes, common among most nomadic groups who have used wheat in their cooking. Flat bread is consumed by the Tuaregs of the North-Africa, Bedouins, Sinai peninsula, and all over Central Asia, Georgia, Armenia, and Azerbaijan. Native American Indians used corn instead of wheat. Colombian and Venezuelan arepa, Salvadorean pupusa, Mexican tortilla are all its relatives, also made of corn, and often come with a spread on top, made of meat and/or vegetables, or any other spreadable paste.

American bagel is structurally a variation of pizza, it looks like! However, its ancestor is a Russian bread bublik, brought into the New World by the Jewish immigrants, and then made into a bagel. The original bublik is much larger in size, and has relatives all over Central Asia, where it does not usually come with a spread.

Folded dishes

A perfect example of a folded dish is a Mexican taco. But how many people know that Azerbaijan is proud of its qutabs, which structurally are the same thing. Is this a coincidence or a practice that spread all over the world with human migration? Flat bread is likely to have been a spread practice, but folding bread with a filling could have easily been independently invented. Someone must study this subject to find out.

Encased dishes

A folded dish with a filling can be sealed, and we get something encased. If you take a soft taco and seal its edges, you will technically get an Italian calzone, a Russian pirozhok or pelmen, Ukrainian varenik, or a Chinese potsticker.

Rolled dishes

A roll is structurally a pizza that has been rolled into a roll. Classical rolled dishes are a thing of the past now. It is rare to see them anymore. However, in the beginning of the 21st century a variation of a roll—a wrap—has become very popular, probably because of the increasing popularity of the Mexican burrito, which is a classic among wraps. Some examples of ancient wraps are Middle-Eastern dolma, which is rice with spices or even ground meat, wrapped in grape leaves, and baked. Ukrainian golubtsi is a variation of this dish.

Here, cooked rice is mixed with raw ground meat, half and half, plus spices, wrapped in raw cabbage leaves, and baked.

Rolls are different from wraps in how the filling is distributed. In rolls, the filling is equally distributed over a tougher ingredient, and the whole thing is evenly rolled into a roll. In a wrap, the filling is kept mostly together, while the cover is wrapped over it. A croissant is probably a classic roll, but with many layers and no filling. Its ancestor is the Indian latcha paratha, is related to the ancient Egyptian ftir, which is a close relative of Italian lasagna. Another example of a roll is a meat roll: thin pieces of meat covered with cheese and herbs, rolled and baked. A Russian poppy seed sweet roll is thin dough with a spread of poppy seed paste on top, rolled and baked. An American cinnamon roll— is a great example of a sweet roll, too. A croissant, after all--is a roll too..

Sandwich

A sandwich is similar to a roll in that it has a filling and covers. On the other hand, a sandwich probably was born from a spread dish: two pizza structures coming together, looking at each other.

A hamburger is probably the most famous sandwich. In the old world, a sandwich is usually open-face—with a structure of a pizza. In the Soviet Russia, bread with butter spread on top was the sandwich. In the US and all over Europe, open face sandwich is still consumed, and bread and butter are served with most meals. In Southern Europe, bread is served with olive oil—an extension of a sandwich, albeit a weak one. The filling in a sandwich could be anything, really, even ice cream. In the Philippines, there is an ice cream sandwich, made with soft hamburger bread! Have you noticed how some people fold a particularly flappy piece of pizza? That is technically a fold, but functionally—a sandwich. A pizza is an open-face sandwich, after all!

Hand-held sandwiches as a whole meal certainly in an invention of the new world, although there are some Japanese varieties of rice sandwiches as well. Although, they seem to be more of a stuffed rice variation than a true sandwich. Philly cheese steak sandwich, Cuban sandwich, and a good old ice cream sandwich—they are all sandwiches we know, and many of us—love.

Stuffed dishes

Stuffed dishes are very popular around the world. Scottish haggis, Polish kielbasa, America stuffed turkey, Mexican tamales, Hong Kong stuffed sticky rice, Egyptian mah'shi—they are all stuffed dishes.

Almost any food item can be stuffed, as long as it has or can be shaped into a round form. Some of the most popular foods for stuffing are bell peppers, large mushrooms, zucchini, apples, tomatoes, but also chicken, turkey and even beef. In

Asia—it is sticky rice. In Ukraine, there is a stuffed mashed potato dish called lezhni.

Toppings

Toppings are decorative, and are a relatively new human invention. Dry powders (dusting with sugar or cocoa powder) and chopped (nuts peanuts in Thai, caramelized onion, green onion, croutons on soup), cherry on top,—are all examples. Presentation is extremely important in the aesthetic experience of a meal, and toppings endow a food creation with a quality of being pristine and untouched. There is nothing less appetizing than sloppily served food that looks over-handled and overcooked. And a topping ensures an illusion of virginity.

Drink mixes

Spices, honey, and herbs were used as medicine from the beginning of human history, and they have arrived in the modern world in the form of drinks for enjoyment and recreation. Even alcoholic drinks have tincture origins—herbal extracts, preserved in alcohol. Herbal teas are still consumed, but their medicinal properties are often overlooked in favor of fashion—that is what health-conscious people drink, but why? No one knows, and many people don't really care.

One modern drink variation involves bubbly water, although bubbly water is naturally found in springs around the world—it is usually salty, and has been used for medicinal purposes. A modern bubbly drink is usually sweet, with a base of a fruit juice, extract, or some other sweetener. It could be easily made of raw cold pressed fruit juice and bubbly water, with supporting ingredients such as honey or xylitol. It is interesting that coffee and tea do not usually come in a bubbly form! Mexican agua fresca is still water with added fruit juice and a sweetener, but no one adds water to a juice, usually, unless it is bubbly water. A smoothie is also a new invention: a mixture of fruit and other ingredients, blended to a consistency that is liquid enough to be sucked through a straw. Usually made of sweet ingredients, avocado can also be added.

Juice from the trees, like birch tree juice, is known mostly in Europe, but is a rarity in the USA and the rest of the world. Boiled fresh berries in plenty of water are called mors in Russia, while dried fruit, boiled with plenty of water is called kompot. Fermented drinks made of milk, whey, honey, or anything that contains sugar and can be fermented, are also ancient. Beer was produced in the Ancient Egypt. In Russia, it was honey or molasses that were fermented, and names medovuha and kvas. Fermented ancient drinks had a minuscule amount of alcohol, compared to what we have now, and were not drunk with every meal. The common ancient drink was water, seconded by milk.

The following are formulas for just a few of the best known dishes, consumed around the world, in their many versions.

Soup

A soup is liquid, usually hot, mixed dish. A soup, is one of the oldest human dishes—along with meat cooked over fire—and traditionally contains hot water with anything edible in it. Literally, anything.

Soup =
water +
anything

A traditional hot soup developed in the cold climates of the planet, in order to provide internal heat to the body, which is a savior during prolonged exposure to cold. This is why during extreme temperatures, one is not recommended to drink alcohol, because alcohol brings the heat toward the surface of the body, and away from its core,—or, at least, that is how my father explained it to me. In the holt climates, humans still consumed soups, but they were cold, resembling paste or thin porridge, just the way it is still done in many African countries.

Soup must have developed during the ages when humans were able to create containers to hold and heat the liquid. In the museums around the world, I have seen everything from stone, to clay, to iron containers—those that could be either stood or hung over a fire, long enough for the soup to heat up, without having the container melt. Clay and stone probably predate iron, because iron has to be mined and melted, then shaped appropriately,—all of which required technology of the Iron Age. Stone Age predates Iron Age, and it is true: the earliest cooking tools found around the planet are made of stone or clay. A stone container needs only a harder stone to shape a softer stone into a cavity. Clay vesicle requires not only shaping wet mud, but it needs high heating, in order for that mud to become hard and durable enough to withstand wear and tear, as well as the trial of fire during food preparation.

Water in the formula is an obvious ingredient, but what is "anything?" Anything literally means anything: from eggs, to leafy greens, to mushrooms, to grains, to fruit. Traditionally, however, human food has been savory, and fruit, honey, berries and other naturally sweet products were eaten on their own, without adding them into main dishes. Sweat-and-sour is a rather modern invention. Historically, humans have consumed what is essentially ketogenic diet, which is by definition savory, because it involves minimum carbohydrates and barely any sweets. It was so until the advent of agriculture, when humans started storing grains and using them as a quick source of energy. In Eastern

Europe, it is still customary to eat everything with bread—no matter what it is. In Northern Africa, and especially among Berbers of Algeria, bread is eaten even with things that, to some, would be unthinkable to pair with it: like potatoes and potato chips.

In all of Asia and Eastern Europe, soup is still considered the main dish, and not an optional side, as it is in the West. In Thailand, soup is street food, available everywhere, and eaten virtually by everyone, even the tourists. My grandmother always told me that soup, eaten first thing in the morning is what would keep my skin smooth and of healthy color, and she was right. Except, soup is hard to cook in the morning, especially, living a western lifestyle.

In the West, the soup has acquired a cold variation. A cold soup is unheard of in the East—it just defeats the purpose! In the East, a soup is considered an essential heating mechanism for the body, but in the West—it is more of an accessory to a meal. Another difference between a Western and Eastern soup is consistency. In the East, a soup is primarily hot liquid with chunks of food in it, often involving a protein, such as meat or chicken, and vegetables. In the West, besides possibly being cold, a soup could be a thicker paste, really, of different foods blended together. As I have grown up with somewhat Eastern taste, the first time I had to try a blended could soup, it was hard to stomach. Well, the key to a cold or hot blended soup is minimal ingredients that produce a pleasant color and smell, so as to avoid looking like vomit. I will allow myself to say that.

The greatest test of my cultural tolerance took place in Sri Lanka. There is a dish there called kottu roti, which is almost literally a mix of every ingredient one can find, laying round in the kitchen: meat or chicken, tomato puree, cheese, macaroni, cabbage, eggs, and could contain more. In any case, it is all mixed together and finely chopped. That was hard to like, but what consoled me was knowing that for so many people—it was a delicacy and a source of enjoyment. Well, that is what makes life interesting! Especially interesting, when one realizes that this dish, kottu roti, is directly related to pad thai—a well loved dish of Thailand. It is most certainly related to the Far-Eastern fried rice, the only difference being rice.

Then, there is a variation of a soup made of lentils, which by its very nature—a paste. As lentils boil, they disintegrate into a thicker or thinner paste, depending on the content of water. This soup probably has its roots in India, where it is still a staple dish. This lentil paste is often treated as a base liquid, and chunks of other foods are added: like potatoes, tomatoes, or even cheese.

There is a clear continuum in dishes, based on their liquid content. Soup has the most liquid. If the liquid in soup is reduced, it becomes a stew. A stew is really just a thick soup. Stews are traditionally made of meat and vegetables, just the like earliest soups known to humanity. If the liquid is further reduced—we basically come back to kottu roti, pad thai, and fried rice family of dishes. In fact, it is a very wide extended family that includes some of the most well spread and ancient dishes that have literally taken over the world: Central Asian plov, Indian biryani, Spanish paella, fried rice, and Egyptian kosheri.

Central Asian plov is a nomadic dish, where lamb meat is cooked with carrots and rice, starting as soup, and cooked down, until it is a solid dish. Indian biryani has the same essential structure, and so does Spanish paella—except there, seafood is used. Egyptian kosheri is macaroni, rice, tomato paste, topped with caramelized onions.

My favorite soup is mushroom soup with barley. It is a hot chunky soup, which, if you boil it down, will become an accompaniment to complete the standard meal trio of carbohydrates, protein and vegetables.

What is the oldest real dish humans ever cooked? I think, it was the soup.

Salad

A salad is a somewhat wet, usually cold, and mixed dish. A salad has to be defined in cultural terms. What comes to mind when we think of a salad in western hemisphere? In the west, the most basic definition of salad is a mix of raw vegetables, especially if they are green and leafy, and small enough to easily fit into one's semi-opened mouth. In the east, a salad is virtually never made of leafy greens, but of finer chopped greens, leaves, vegetables, mushrooms, and just about anything else.

Raw leafy salad =
leafy greens +
toppings +
salad dressing

My favorite leafy greens: arugula, watercress.

Possible toppings: berries, seeds, nuts, lentils, fruit, vegetables, nutritional yeast.

Salad dressing =
oil +
vinegar +
spice

Usually, salad dressing oils are fluid, the best ones being olive, toasted sesame, and peanut. Oils that solidify at room temperature, such as coconut and palm, can also be used, but in cold salads, they will stay solid and will not spread well, creating an unpleasant texture. There are many types of vinegar, especially in France, where such varieties as orange and raspberry, are popular.

By spice I mean almost anything: just like in the United States, when the label says "spice" that could be a lot of things. In a salad, my favorite "spice" is nutritional yeast, but it could be molasses, another sweetener, salt, lemon juice, truffle or garlic

74

paste, a paste made of olives or sun dried tomatoes, mustard, a real spice such as turmeric, or anything that will blend well into something liquid that can be poured over leafy greens and then will spread around them. Large seeds, for example, such as pumpkin seeds, are better not admixed into a salad dressing, but added separately.

In the Mediterranean region, especially Greece, salads usually involve tomatoes, onions and cucumbers, cut in large chunks. Central Asian salads include both the Mediterranean tomato-onion-cucumber combination, but many of their salads are made with cooked vegetables, and also include proteins.

There are as many cooked vegetable salads as there are vegetables, but there are 4 vegetables that seem to be popular across cultures: bell pepper, eggplant, potato, beat, and greens. Bell pepper salad is basically minced bell pepper that is roasted or fried into smooth consistency, and is found everywhere in the Middle East, Armenia,

Azerbaijan, Georgia, and as far as Ukraine, Russia, and Eastern Europe. Paprika spice goes well with it.

Cooked eggplant salad is basically the same as cooked bell pepper salad, but a spice that goes well with it is fennel. Eggplants salad can be prepared by cutting eggplant into pieces and then cooking it to smooth consistency, or preserving some chunks. Smooth consistency is what we find in baba ganuj dish, prevalent all over Middle East, and even in China—I tried it in none other than a tiny cafe in Zhang Jia Jie—deep into mainland China.

Potato salad is one that seems to have conquered the world. In Eastern Europe, they call it by a French word "olivier", and in the US—it is just simply potato salad. At its base, it is cooked potatoes and mayonnaise. In the post-Soviet countries, it also contains pickled cucumbers, sausage, carrots, and eggs. Some people even add onions. Yes, it sounds like a deadly mixture, but it comes out tasty—especially if you are used to it since childhood. It seems that that whole region of the world prefers salads that have a great mixture of ingredients, and can only be rivaled by the Mexican traditional sauces with a famously large number of unique ingredients. Beet salad is also a dish from the post-Soviet region, but with remarkably few ingredients: boiled beets, mayonnaise, and minced garlic. Sometimes, prunes are added.

A salad of cooked greens is probably the oldest human invention, and it is spread all over Africa, Asia, the Caribbean, and Polynesia. There is a great variety of greens that are used: from ferns, to spinach, to kale.

My favorite salads to cook have fresh arugula or watercress as a base, olive or sesame oil and vinegar as a dressing, and avocado, roasted pine nuts, and artichoke hearts.

Curry

Curry is a wet, mixed, hot dish. It is basically a stew with a lot of spice in it. Coconut curry is a stew with a lot of spice, plus coconut cream.

Curry =
vegetables and/or proteins +
oil +
spice

What makes curry not a soup? It's the ratio of solids to liquid in it, for the most part. However, some soups, like Hungarian goulash, are very close to being stews. Stew is a thick soup, and a soup is a very watery stew. There is really no clear border between them.

Usually, a curry starts with a hot oil that cooks the spices, then vegetables or protein, or both, are added. With coconut curries, coconut cream is added toward the end of the cooking

78

process. It all varies by region, but curry as we know it seems to have originated in India, its deeper roots going back to Africa, to the most ancient human migrations. From India, curry travelled to South-East Asia, and now countries such as Thailand, Indonesia, and Malaysia consider curry their national dish.

My favorite curry is, of course, a very simple one. It is chicken chunks, plus toasted sesame seed oil, plus onions and garlic, plus turmeric, paprika, cayenne pepper, cumin, cardamom, cloves, coriander, salt and black pepper. A lot of spice! Toward the end, I add coconut cream into the mixture, keep cooking for a few minutes, and it is ready. It is almost impossible to not do this dish well!

Stir fry

Stir fry is relatively dry, hot, mixed dish. It is basically a stew or a soup, but without the water.

Why is stir fry not just a watery stew? Because the chunks in it must remain springy and crunchy enough to keep it out of the stew category. If they soften, a stir fry can turn into a strange paste that is not a paste, not a stew, and not really a soup. Stir fry is chopped vegetables and/or proteins plus oil, all lightly cooked on high fire, and served immediately.

Stir fry =
vegetables and/or proteins +
oil +
high heat

Stir fry reminds me of soup, because it is the same ingredients, except they are not boiled in water, but just heated. The key to a stir fry is dryness and crunchiness, otherwise it either becomes steamed vegetables or something unintelligible—which is perfectly ok. I cook and eat that all the time! For example, I cook okra like that. Okra is naturally wet and slimy, so it is hard to make it into a true stir fry without very high heat. I use medium heat, and add tomatoes and garlic, plus an olive oil and some water, then cook it until okra is ready—this is the closest to the stir fry I ever make.

Another variation of a stir fry is based on eggs. Eggs are added into the mixture, so that their mass sticks to individual food chunks. Eggs generally act as a glue in food, but in a stir fry—they create an interesting texture.

Fried rice is a type of a stir fry. China is famous for its fried rice. It is rice, cooked accordingly, then stir fried with vegetables, eggs, and spices. I really like the way Egyptians cook their rice. It is one part rice, one and a half part water, a little oil (I use gradeseed oil!), spice, all brought to a boil on high heat, then heat is lowered to the minimum, until all the water evaporates. The grade seed oil makes the rice springy and not sticky. One can also add all kinds of nuts or seeds. Whole caraway or cumin seeds are some of the best. Sesame or black cumin seeds, are also good, but they will color the rice dark. There is a also a variation of this dish, where a little portion of rice is cooked in oil first, until it turns brown, then the rest of rice is added. The resulting rice has two colors.

It is interesting that dessert, as we know it now, has not been a common dish in the ancient times. Honey, fruit and berries were the dessert of the ancients, and I tend to overlook it in my cooking and eating practices. Ice cream is only about a thousand year old dish, and in those remote times, it was the naturally occurring ice, mostly from the mountains, that was used to create it. One type of ice creams deserves a special mention: Turkish dondurma. What makes it special is its texture. It is thick and stretchy, and smooth at the same time. Dondurma is one ancient type of ice cream that has been preserved until modern times, and is the only in the world to include sales and mastic as ingredients. They are the ones that create its spectacular texture. Although dondurma is sold in many neighboring countries, the only place that has assimilated dondurma tradition, is Egypt. It happened during the Ottoman Empire era. Overall, however, a sweet tooth is a luxury only a modern human can entertain.

If we could map traditional dishes of the world, we would see that there are migration patterns, and often what many nations deem to be their national dish, actually, has an older ancestor, and relatives around the world.

The most ancient drink is water, and the youngest drink is a soda. The history of human cooking started with a soup, and ended—with a sandwich. Maybe, we still have new food structures ahead of us.

A food structure does not sound so appetizing, though. Let's hope for a new gustatory creation that titillates all senses and fills us with nutrients, for a good a happy life.

I hope, someone invents one soon.